K-LITERATURE

KOREAN CULTURE NO.8

K-LITERATURE: The Writing World's New Voice

First Published in 2012 by
Korean Culture and Information Service
Ministry of Culture, Sports and Tourism

Phone: 82-2-398-1914~20
Fax: 82-2-398-1882
Website: www.kocis.go.kr

ISBN: 978-89-7375-567-7 04810
ISBN: 978-89-7375-163-1 (set)

Printed in the Republic of Korea

For further information about Korea, please visit:
www.korea.net

K-LITERATURE

The Writing World's New Voice

Contents

LA NOUVELLE
REVUE FRANÇAISE

AVRIL 1998 — N° 543

AVENTURES DU ROMAN

LETTRES
DE CORÉE

PROLOGUE

How much history goes into a single line of writing? A newspaper might need only a few hours to report something that happened earlier that day, but the birthing of a work of literature takes far, far longer. For the present to become history and for history to become the letters of the future requires both great contemplation and eclectic experimentation.

For decades now, people have been working to bring Korea's literary voices to the rest of the world, translating works into different tongues in the hopes of vaulting over the long wait and steep language barrier to connect it with the body of world literature. It is only relatively recently that those efforts have begun to bear fruit, bringing Korean literature into the

Members of Book Club Lisas in San Francisco, which selected
Please Look After Mom as its "book of the month"

overseas spotlight. One precipitating factor has been the boom in Korean
television series and films, part of the so-called "Korean Wave." As these
examples of popular culture were welcomed by global audiences, their
source materials began receiving newfound attention.

This has been evident in more and more countries by the day. Korean
literature was long relegated to the global periphery—a consequence of
language barriers—but with the recent smashing success of Shin Kyung-
sook's book *Please Look After Mom*, more and more works are finding their
way to global readers. Translated versions of Shin's novel have been sold in

Hwang Sok-yong gives a reading of Korean literature at an old bookstore in Stockholm.

31 countries around the world as of 2011, including the United States and the United Kingdom, spearheading a Korean Literature Wave.

The following pages provide an overview of the past and present of Korean literature: the authors, publishers, and translators who played a part in its globalization, as well as the institutional support that helped usher it to its current success. They were written in the hopes that more foreign readers might find their own connections, their own resonances, in the voices now emerging from the Hermit Kingdom.

Chapter One

BREAKING NATIONAL BOUNDARIES AND LANGUAGE BARRIERS

New Faces and Pages in Global Literature

Korea's location at the far eastern end of Asia has historically posed a major obstacle to its literature reaching the outside world, particularly in terms of its relationship with Western society, which is commonly viewed as the center of the literary universe. Further confounding matters is the Korean language's structural dissimilarity to Western tongues—a major factor in its belated arrival before a foreign readership. But steady efforts have been made since the 1980s to reach out and touch the mainstream of world literature, efforts that have largely succeeded in bringing down barriers of language and culture. Today, Korean literature is earning notice around the world, reaching a wider readership than ever before.

One particularly successful example is Shin Kyung-sook's *Please Look After Mom* (2011). This was Korea's first novel ever to crack the *New York Times* bestseller list, with a first edition printing of 100,000 copies.

Shin Kyung-sook (Right) visits a Korean *hanok* house with Robin Desser (Left), her editor at Knopf. Desser described the house as a "beautiful paradox."

Publishing rights were sold in 31 countries, and the book earned selection on a list of 2011's best works of fiction and literature selected by Amazon.com, the world's biggest online bookstore. The American market is seen by many as having the world's most formidable entry barriers: foreign books are a paltry 3%, and foreign literature an even smaller piece of the pie—less than one percent. Shin's book succeeded in cracking it wide open, earning rave reviews for its writing, universal resonance, and mass appeal in the process. It also won its author the 2012 Man Asia Literary Prize, an honor created in 2007 by the Man Group (sponsors of the Man Booker Prize, Britain's most prestigious literary award) to honor writers from the 35 countries of Asia. The result of this has been a flurry of overseas contracts not just for Shin's follow-up to her bestseller, but for other Korean authors, too. Robin Desser, vice president of the American publishing company Knopf, said the book resonated most strongly with overseas readers for the universality of its emotions and its portrayal of the bonds of human affection. Sophie Buchan, an editor at the British publisher Weidenfeld & Nicolson, said she was astonished at the book's universality, calling particular attention to the resonance of Shin's depiction of motherhood and its detailed observations on the growing divide between country parents and their urbanite children.

Early in the 2000s, the Korean writer who garnered the most global attention was Ko Un. Most famous for his poetry collection *Ten Thousand Lives*, Ko was mentioned early on in the decade as a strong contender to win Korea its first Nobel Prize in Literature. High praise indeed, especially since this was a reflection of major figures in world literature taking note of his authorial vision and life, rather than one of the typical fan club drives where readers around the world nominate a local for the award. A monument engraved with his verse was erected in Malaga, Spain; in Australia, *Ten Thousand Lives* was put on the required reading list or used as a text at various middle and high schools. The poems in this collection, which tell the stories of countless ordinary Koreans enduring poverty and war, drew major praise for their meticulous renderings, like thousands of painstaking portraits. Another collection by Ko, *Flowers of a Moment*, was praised by *Dagens Nyheter*, a leading daily in Sweden (the country that bestows Nobel Prizes), for the richness of its poetry, which

Ko Un's collection *Awakening from Sleep* was praised by major German media upon its 2008 publication.

Lee Seung-u's work has been translated into numerous languages.

was described as "all-encompassing." The reader, the newspaper wrote, felt embraced in the great bosom of humanity.

Lee Seung-u

The literati and readers of Europe— France in particular, but also Germany— were quicker than the English-speaking world to take note of Korean literature. After their publication in France in the early 2000s, the works of Lee Seung-u and Hwang Sok-yong were singled out for heavy praise by the local media and readers. Indeed, both were under consideration in the foreign literature category of the Prix Femina, one of the country's major literary awards. The 2000 publication of Lee's novel *The Reverse Side of Life* in French translation was met with great interest by the French press. Major newspapers like *Le Monde, Le Figaro*, and *La Croix* dedicated major space to it on their culture pages, spotlighting it in headlines and feature articles. The novel went on to reach the final stages of consideration for the Prix Femina's foreign fiction category. *Reverse* is a profound exploration of the meaning of writing itself, using a novel-within-a-novel structure in which a first-person narrator writes the biography of a novelist named Park Gil-bu. *Le Monde* was lavish in its praise, saying the book was a moving and weighty expression from a quiet and serious soul that was certain to capture the interest of true devotees of literature.

In 2009, another novel by Lee, *The Private Lives of Plants*, was added to the Folio series, a collection of works by noted foreign authors that is carefully selected by the top French publisher Gallimard. It was also

Hwang Sok-yong gives a reading from *The Old Garden* at the Stockholm bookstore Rönnells Antikvariat.

included in a list of the ten most notable foreign novels by Fnac. It reached #11 on a French Booksellers' Association list of new novel sales, providing clear evidence of its strong reception from French readers. The book itself is an elegantly crafted story about the lives of people living like trees—"avatars of thwarted love"—in an animalistic, dog-eat-dog society. J. M. G. Le Clézio, a Nobel laureate, recommended making a film version to a Korean director he met. *Le Figaro* praised it as a tremendous novel with rich and powerful imagery that brought the mythical dimensions of love to the fore.

Hwang Sok-yong has earned praise in France as one of Korea's most engaged authors. Three of his most prominent works—*A Chronology of Mr. Han*, *The Guest*, and *Shim Chong*—were published there by Zulma, with the first having come out in 2002. *The Old Garden* was selected as

(Left) French edition of Hwang Sok-yong's *Shim Chong*
(Right) German edition of *The Old Garden*

a book of the year by *Le Monde*. Amid this acclaim, a contract was signed for *Mr. Han* and *Shim Chong*, as well as *On the Road to Sampo*, to be published as a series by Seuil, which ranks alongside Gallimard as one of the country's leading publishing houses. *Shim Chong* is now in print.

In Germany, a number of Hwang's books were released by the leading publisher DTV around the time of a 2005 event to honor Korea at the Frankfurt International Book Fair. In Sweden, the prominent publisher Albert Bonniers Förlag released a 2011 translation of *The Old Garden*, declaring that the author "wrestles with the big questions: love, life, resistance. He limns a warm portrait of a generation in Korea who had to give up their youth, their freedom, even their lives for the dream of a better future."

Other authors have also reached a worldwide readership. In 2011, contracts were signed to publish Gong Ji-yeong's *Our Time of Happiness* in 11 countries, including Great Britain, China, Japan, Italy, and France. Han Kang's *Vegetarian* earned rave reviews from critics in Japan and Vietnam. That same year, Kim Ae-ran's *My Palpitating Life*, a bestseller back home, had contracts finalized for publication in France, Japan, China, and Taiwan. Every day, more and more works of Korean literature are breaking national boundaries and language barriers.

This globalizing generation benefited greatly from the pioneering efforts of past writers like Younghill Kang, Li Mi-rok, and Richard E. Kim. Although they did not write in Korean, they did share their country—its characteristic sentiments, its historical situation—at a time when world readers were unfamiliar with the existence of Korea itself, let alone its literary tradition. Their work has not been a part of the recent translation push, but they are key figures who warrant reexamination in any study of Korea's literary history.

Younghill Kang, a native of the town of Hungwon in North Hamgyeong province (part of North Korea today), lived from 1898 to 1972. Works like *The Grass Roof* (1931) and *East Goes West* (1937) were well received by

readers in the United States; UN World once lauded him as the most famous living Korean. *The Grass Roof* was particularly successful, earning him Guggenheim Award and Book of the Century honors and being published in translation in around a dozen countries, including Germany, France, Yugoslavia, and Czechoslovakia. The book skillfully depicts the beauty of simple Korean lives in nature, while also incorporating elements of contemporary society and history: the devastation wrought on these lives by Japan's invasion and plundering,

Younghill Kang and his book *The Grass Roof*

and the reasons for the inevitability of the country's 1919 independence movement.

Li Mi-rok (1899–1950) was the only Korean writer to write in German. His autobiographical novel *The Yalu River Flows* was published in 1946 by the Munich publisher Piper. Set during the period of historical upheaval leading up to Japan's colonization of Korea, the book was hugely popular with readers and literati—it was even used in a German high school textbook. It was later released in English translation, first in Great Britain (1954) and then in the United States (1956).

Richard E. Kim (1932–2009) told the story of a preacher in wartime Korea in his book *The Martyred* (1964), a bestseller that was lauded by the *New York Times* as the successor to the great moral and psychological tradition of Dostoevsky and Camus. In 1965, it was adapted into a film by the Korean director Yu Hyun-mok; in 1967, Kim was named as a candidate for the Nobel Prize in Literature.

In addition to these authors, Kim Yu-jeong also made a splash in France with his short story collection *A Rainy Spell*, which sold out in its first printing and went down in history as the best-selling work of Korean literature in such a short period of time.

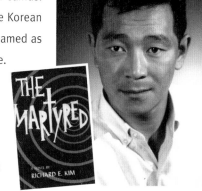

(Top) Li Mi-rok and his *The Yalu River Flows*
(Bottom) Richard E. Kim and his *The Martyred*

Foreign Perspectives on Korean Literature

It holds a special meaning for a country to have distinguished overseas literary journals with a longstanding tradition and readership focus on that country's writers and writing in their pages. As Korean literature has gained in stature overseas, it has come under the spotlight at more and more noted overseas media.

The first example of this came in 1996, when the German literary quarterly *Die Horen* dedicated its winter edition to Korean letters. This journal has a proud history of 180 editions since being launched in 1955 by the literary publishing agency of the same name. In addition to having regular local readers, it is also distributed to major libraries and literature/arts institutes in 25 countries. Sprawling over 216 pages, the special edition covered the full gamut of Korean writers active since the 1960s — the so-called "Hangeul generation." They included pieces by 27 figures from the Korean literary world: eleven poets (among them Jung Hyeon-jong and Kim Ji-ha), ten fiction writers (including Yi Chong-jun, Yi Mun-yol, and Oh Jung-hee), two playwrights (Ham Sae-deok and Yi Gang-baek), three critics, and one essayist.

In France, where interest in Korean literature dates to the early 1990s, journals have been even more attentive to Korean literature on their pages. *Poésie* has had two special editions on Korean verse, in 1999 and 2012. Today considered one of the most prestigious poetry

The French literary journal *Poésie* did a special issue on Korean poetry in May 2012. It also covered Korean poetry in 1999.

journals in the country, *Poésie* was launched in June 1977 by the Belin publishing company, and had such outstanding French and Francophone poets as Michel Deguy serving on its editorial board. Its 1999 edition shared the work of 12 leading Korean poets, including Yi Sang, Kim Chun-su, Ko Un, and Ki Hyung-do, providing a first close look at Korean poetry for many French readers. The May 2012 edition, entitled "Poésie-Corée," was a comprehensive treatment showing the different trends at play in Korean verse, from contemporary poetry veterans like Ko, Moon Jeong-hui, and Lee Seong-bok to established and emerging poets representative of the current work being done. The 27 poets were introduced according to five major themes: freedom, struggle, life, change, and encounters.

A particularly historic moment for Korean literature came when Europe's two most prestigious literary journals, *La Nouvelle Revue Française (NRF)* and *Europe*, each did special editions on it. The former, a quarterly published by world-renowned French publisher Gallimard, focused on Korea for its spring and summer 2008 editions in a feature titled "Lettres de Corée." Founded in 1908 and considered by many a cradle of 20th century French literature and thought, with such luminaries as André Gide, Paul Valéry, and Marcel Proust serving on its editorial board, this storied journal was now training its focus on the diversity of Korean literature.

The spring edition featured a critical overview of Korean contemporary literary history by Seoul National University professor Park Sung-chang and an essay titled "Jeong and Han, Love and Revenge" by Nobel laureate J. M. G. Le Clézio, along with works by 14 Korean authors, including Hwang Sun-won's short story "Theory of Masculine Regression" and Ko Un's "Flowers of a Moment." In the summer edition, the pages included another 16 works, including Kim Hoon's novella *Cremation* and poet Ki Hyung-do's

(Left) *NRF*'s 585th issue in 2008 spotlighted Korean literature.
(Rignt) *NRF* editor-in-chief Michel Braudeau visited Korea in 2008.

"The Black Leaf in My Mouth."

The journal declared that Korean literature had great potential, despite being relatively unknown in France compared to the work coming from China or Japan, and called the special editions an opportunity to experience a modern literature with a surprisingly broad spectrum. It also linked characteristics of Korean literature with the country's rapid industrialization, noting signs of the latter in the former. This stood to reason, it said, since the writers experienced different eras—changes that had taken a long time to unfold in French literature were occurring at a rapid and dynamic pace in Korea.

Le Clézio, a member of the *NRF* editorial board, singled out young female writers like Han Kang and Kim Ae-ran for particular acclaim, saying he would not be surprised to see either of them winning the Nobel Prize a few decades on. Korean literature, he said, was as dynamic as Korea itself, and the themes of its younger writers were novel things that went unobserved in France. His hope, he added, was that the special edition would be an opportunity for French readers who only associated Korea with war to encounter a new facet of the country.

Listed in the Arts & Humanities Citation Index (A&HCI) as a literary academic journal, *Europe* printed a Korean Writer Special in its May 2010 edition, focusing its attention on the current state of Korean fiction. The criticism journal's founding in 1923 was spearheaded by Romain Rolland, one of France's leading writers, with the participation of Louis Aragon, Paul Eluard, Jean Guéhenno, Antoine Vietz, and others. For its special edition, it included works by and commentary on six Korean writers born in the years since 1950, including Kim Yeon-su, Lee Seung-u, Jeong I-Hyeon, and Pyun Hye-young. It focused on Korean fiction that had been published since 1987 (the year of South Korea's successful transition to democracy). Presenting the work in three categories—new reflections, new imagination, and new writing—it offered critical commentary on each trend and selected representative writers to excerpt from and introduce their major works.

The French literary journal *Europe* did a "Korean Writer Special" for its May 2010 edition.

In recent years, journals in the United States and Asia have also begun publishing special features on

The American bimonthly literary journal *World Literature Today* dedicated a 16-page article to Korean literature in its January/February edition for 2010.

Introduction:
Korean Literature, Then and Now

Jonathan C. Stalling & Eun-Gwi Chung

In Yoo Hiseok's article "Promoting Korean Literature?" (page 33), he questions our ability to assert the existence of a single "modern Korean literature." He notes the radical differences between two very distinct Korean nation-states—North Korea (DPRK) and South Korea (ROK)—while simultaneously offering examples of contemporary writing that may point us toward a "twinned" sense of what constitutes modern Korean literature. Yet also implicit in that question mark is the acknowledgment of how much remains for English readers to learn about the richness of contemporary Korean literature. Understanding the full arc of modern Korean literature's genuine complexities will require a brief look back at some basic contours of the century leading up to the present moment.

The modern period of Korean literature can be said to have begun toward the end of what is known as the Korean Enlightenment (1896–1910), yet due to Japan's annexation of Korea in 1910, most of Korea's early modernist writing took place under the continual repression of imperial rule that lasted until the end of World War II. Although seriously hampered by Japan's explicit political and cultural oppression, which brutally suppressed Korean language, literature, and culture, Korean modernism took root during this period and even flourished at times. The first such period began a few years after the crushing crackdown on the Korean Independence Movement (1919), as Japan sought to improve its public relations both inside Korea and internationally by easing restrictions on publications and allowing the establishment of literary groups. The decades that followed saw the founding of numerous literary magazines and the rise of popular poets like Kim Sowŏl (1902–34), whose poem "Azaleas" is still memorized throughout Korea today, and high modernists such as Yi Sang (1910–37), whose

cosmopolitan and sophisticated modernist poetics were unmatched in his day and set the bar very high for experimental writing in the twenty-first century. Yet this early modernist period also saw the genesis of the Korean Artists Proletarian Federation, which pursued an explicitly socialist agenda. Although the group's writings were banned in South Korea until after the 1988 Olympics in Seoul, the trend toward political solidarity (especially that of the left) remained a major feature of modern Korean literature until the 1990s.

Most Americans are aware of the tumult caused by both the Japanese colonial period and the brutality of the Korean War (1950–53), but few are knowledgeable about the three decades of domestic political oppression initiated by the U.S. Army military government in Korea (USAMGIK), which worked hard to suppress leftist activity. A succession of U.S.-backed dictatorial governments (known as the First, Second, Third, Fourth, and Fifth Republics of Korea) continued to severely suppress leftist activity, culminating in the brutal massacre of hundreds of students who partook in the Kwangju Uprising during the 1980s. These three decades saw the rise of explicitly political literary groups such as the National Literature Movement, and most writers publicly allied themselves with oppositional politics or political groups.

Two poets whose work exemplifies the power of poetry in these tumultuous decades are Kim Chiha and Ko Ŭn. Though other poets like Kim Suyŏng managed to capture the spirit of the years directly following the Korean War, the work of Kim Chiha and Ko Ŭn captured the imagination of the postwar years. Kim Chiha's compelling political poetry became the anthems of student protests. Ko Ŭn's large and powerful body of work transcends the politics of his era but still retains the charge of his high-profile political commitments.

Perspectives on Contemporary Korean Literature

Korean literature. While it may not have been an exclusive "Korea issue," Korean writing did receive a 16-page article in one U.S. journal. *World Literature Today*, published by the University of Oklahoma to introduce overseas writing, was the one to dedicate this much space to Korean literature in its January / February edition for 2010, covering the different eras and generations at work and introducing leading works such as Shin Kyung-sook's *Please Look After Mom*. In its introduction, the piece points to the 1980s as the dividing line between two eras of Korean literature: a national writing movement in the preceding modern era, and a broader discourse of "the nation" afterwards, in which writers began focusing more on everyday lives and personal issues.

Meanwhile, the leading Chinese literary monthly *Zuojia* featured an exclusive on contemporary Korean writing in its April 2010 edition, with a cover design featuring the faces of prominent writers. This journal, which has been published on a monthly basis since 1956 by the Chinese government (with more than 490 issues as of 2011), is considered required reading by local writers, with such leading lights as Mo Yan (the 2012 Nobel Prize winner in literature) and Wang Anyi publishing their work in

its pages. The Korea edition included Chinese translations of 16 works of short fiction by different Korean writers, along with 28 works of poetry by 12 poets. It was considered highly unusual in the Chinese literary world for such a prominent medium to devote an entire issue to Korean writing.

Zuojia, China's leading literature monthly, did a special issue on modern Korean literature in April 2010.

People Go Wild for
Korean Literature

Blogging

Since 2006, an American blogger without any connection to the government or a Korean translation organization has been hard at work bringing Korean literature to readers in English translation. Charles Montgomery is a professor in the English literature department at Dongguk University in Seoul. A former marketing director and editor who majored in literature, he was first introduced to Korean writing by a native Korean teacher friend in the United States. Dismayed at the lack of awareness overseas, he and his friend started an English-language blog called "Korean Modern Literature in Translation" (www. ktlit.com), and the rest was history. As he worked to introduce Korean writers and writing to the world, Montgomery discovered just how little information was out there in English, and began a project uploading details on major Korean writers and their work to Wikipedia. In his eyes, a number of Korean works are worthy of Nobel Prize. In particular, he singled out Ko Un, Park Wan-seo, Yi Mun-yol, and Park Gyeong-ri as deserving of international renown.

(Left) Charles Montgomery
(Right) The blog Korean Modern Literature in Translation

Literature Majors

The first decade of the 21st century brought a major increase in the number of non-Koreans studying Korean literature in Korea's graduate schools. Some of them fell in love with Korea while visiting the country; others came as exchange students and stayed to finish a master's degree in Korean literature. Andrew Krebsbach, 27, is one of the latter: a graduate student in Korean language and literature at Sogang University, he is especially passionate about the country's writing.

In his view, Korean literature is an important avenue for understanding Korea and its different cultures. As an example, he noted the presence of sirens in books written during the 1960s and 1970s. "Everyone runs inside when they hear them," he said. "I've never had any experience like that in Korea. So by reading the books, I could get some indirect sense of what life in Korea was like at the time."

Krebsbach recently read Kim Seung-ok's book *Seoul, Winter 1964*. "The protagonist's wife dies, but he has no money for the funeral," he said. "So he sells the body for 4,000 won. Today, that will buy you a cup of coffee. There's also a scene where they're eating sparrows on skewers. It was interesting to discover things like that."

One of Krebsbach's favorite works of Korean fiction is Choi In-hun's *The Square*. As he read about the main character Lee Myeong-jun's life, he found himself asking existential questions—what he wanted to do, what kind of person he wanted to be. This was during his university days, when he was worried about his future, and he recognized something familiar in the Myeong-jun character's wandering between "the square" and "the secret room."

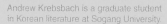

Andrew Krebsbach is a graduate student in Korean literature at Sogang University.

Chapter Two

A HISTORY OF **KOREAN LITERATURE**

Elan and Elation (Pre-"Enlightenment" Korea)

Korea's classic literature affords a rich portrait of the lives and loves of the Korean people, their dreams and their desires. Their values, unchanging over the passage of years, seem to speak directly to us. It is writing that expresses love, affection, sadness, and joy that are common to all humankind, but it also captures the human being in his or her encounters with nature and communion with the universe.

The classics are a treasure trove of human imagination, contemplation, and narration. They weather the storms of time to reemerge, alive and vibrant, in the here and now. All the different patterns of human existence seem to surge and billow within them. As such, they offer a prime opportunity for world readers to see the way Koreans have lived over the centuries and the love of elegance and letters imbued in that way of living.

(Left) "Hwangjoga" was printed in the Goryeo era record *Samguk Sagi* (1145). (Right) Orioles

The first recorded work of lyric poetry is "Hwangjoga" ("Song of the Orioles"), written by Yuri, the second king of Goguryeo (37 BC–AD 668). Dating from the year 17 BC, a the king laments a lost love as he watches the warm frolicking of a pair of orioles:

> *Lightly flying orioles,*
> *Male and female, show love to one another;*
> *but lonesome as I am,*
> *With whom shall I go home?*

> - "Hwangjoga" ("Song of the Orioles")

The story goes that Yuri tried to win back the lover who had left him one day. Unsuccessful in his attempts, he was on his way back to Goguryeo when he saw orioles gathering as he stood under the shade of a tree. The lonesome king thought back to his lost love and composed the plaintive lyric on the spot. "Hwangjoga" is considered one of Korea's first examples of lyric poetry as a form of individual expression—as opposed to a primeval art form of a collective and religious nature—and is of interest in literary history for the way it captures the simple sentiments of a person living in ancient times.

The *hyangga* folk song was the dominant literary form during the Silla era (57 BC–AD 935), a period marked by a strong tradition of Buddhist culture. Many of these songs were composed by monks, but there were also versions written by ordinary people. One of the most representative is "Heonhwaga" ("Flower Dedication Song"), whose title refers to the dedication of a flower to a beautiful lady. In it, a noblewoman is moved by the sight of a beautiful royal azalea on a seaside cliff; a passing old man risks his life to cut it down and give it to the woman, singing the words of the early 8th century lyric as he does so:

> *Allow me to release my cow*
> *Beside that red rock;*
> *If you are not embarrassed by me,*
> *I'll cut flowers to give you.*

> - "Heonhwaga" ("Flower Dedication Song")

Lee Man-ik's painting *Flower Dedication Song* shows a scene from the poem "Heonhwaga."

© MKCOLLECTION

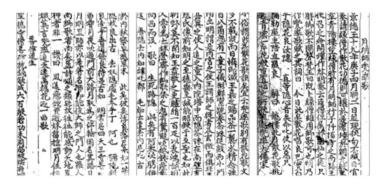

"Jemangmaega" was printed in the Goryeo era record *Samguk Yusa* (c. 1281)

The words express the old man's pureness of feeling: though he may only be a stranger herding a cow, he says, if the woman is not embarrassed of him, he is more than willing to risk his life on the steep cliff to hand her the blossom.

Another example of the *hyangga* form is the mid-8th century work "Jemangmaega" ("Requiem for the Dead Sister"), written by the Silla era high priest Wolmyeong as he grieved the death of his sister. Plunged into sadness over her sudden passing, he realizes that like the leaves scattered by the autumn wind, he and his sister were fated to be born on the same branch but would not know where they would drift:

Was it because you feared that this
Was the crossroads of life and death
That you left without a word of farewell?

Like leaves blown here and there
By early autumn winds,
Born of the same branch
We know not where we are going.
Ah, till we meet in Amitabha's land
I will wait, cultivating my mind.

-"Jemangmaega" ("Requiem for a Dead Sister")

Korean literature began developing during the Three Kingdoms and Unified Silla eras, a period that saw an influx of institutions and cultural forms from China. The leading form of lyric poetry in the Goryeo era (918–1392) is called the Goryeo *gayo* (song), the most famous example of which is "Samogok" ("Song for Thoughts of Mother"). This piece, whose author and time of composition remain unknown, likens a mother to a sickle and a father to a hoe: both are blades, but the hoe cuts less deeply. In other words, though a father is a parent, he cannot prize his child as a mother does. With this verse, the author declares that there is no love in human existence as absolute as a mother's love:

Though a hoe too has a blade,
It cannot cut as well as a sickle.
Though a father is also a parent,
Wi deong deo dung syeong
He cannot love like a mother does.
Ah! My dear, you cannot love like a mother does.

- "Samogok" ("Song for Thoughts of Mother")

The Goryeo era saw a great deal of fusion in Korean literature as a result of the introduction of various educational institutions and the *gwageo*, civil service examination. A founding myth of Goryeo was created from the previous era's folktale traditions, and so these Three Kingdom stories assumed a firm place in the canon. Just as the Brothers Grimm created fairy tales from folklore, so too did Goryeo's writers harness the stories of the people, transforming them into something new.

Chong Chi-sang, one of the leading writers of this era, was recognized from childhood as a genius at Chinese poetry. His skills were said to be so great that according to a popular bit of "unofficial history", he composed a verse at the age of five upon seeing a heron on the river ("As though someone has taken a white brush and written a 'Z' on the river waters"). Chong was deeply interested in the ideas of Lao-tze and well versed in Buddhism, while possessing great skill in both painting and writing (in the traditional society of the day, people who were talented at poetry, prose,

and painting were recognized as *munsa*, or "men of letters"). His most famous work is "Songin" ("Seeing Someone Off"), in which he sings the sorrow of parting as he gazes over a river:

> *The grass is deep green on the long banks after rain.*
> *Having seen my love off at Nampo, my song is sad.*
> *How can the Daedong River ever run dry?*
> *Each year, tears of separation add another blue wave.*

- "Songin" ("Seeing Someone Off")

Korea also has a strong tradition of literature by women. Historically, women had few opportunities to become literate, and no opportunities at all to sit for the *gwageo* examination that selected the most talented individuals to run the country. This fact makes the tradition of women's

Monghon, a collection of poetry and prose by Yi Ok-bong

writing all the more rare and valuable. Prominent female poets include Shin Saimdang (whose face graces today's 50,000-won bill), Heo Nanseolheon, Yi Ok-bong, and Hwang Jin-i. Also a talented painter, Shin was the mother of Yi Yul-gok, one of Korea's most noted philosophers; Heo was the sister of Heo Kyun, author of the first novel written in Korea's Hangeul writing system.

Yi Ok-bong deserves special mention for her poetry, characterized by a gusto and clarity not typically associated with women's verse. Active in the mid-Joseon era, she was said to be renowned for her poetry as far away as China. Her most famous work is the mid-16th century "Monghon" ("Dream Spirit"):

> *I am asking you, how you are doing?*
> *There is so much of my sorrow on the moonlit silk window.*
> *Half the stone path before your house would have turned to sand,*
> *had I allowed my sprit in my dream to leave its footprints on that path.*

> -"Monghon" ("Dream Sprit")

Hwang Jin-i, who was a *gisaeng* (a type of female entertainer) during the Joseon era (1392–1910), remains a figure of fascination today, appearing regularly in historical television programs and films. Her plaintive love lyrics from the early 17th century are often recited to this day:

Illustration of Hwang Jin-i by the painter Chang Sun-hwan

I'll take a slice of long winter's night,
keep it curled under a quilt of spring wind,
then unfurl it on the night my beloved comes

Sijo by Hwang Jin-i

Indeed, *gisaeng* poets accounted for most of the three-stanza *sijo* poems written by women during the Joseon era. Their ardent and truthful expressions of love and longing were conveyed with a delicacy of feeling that only a woman could supply. These poets also contributed to development of poetic language with their sophistication of technique and well-tuned ear for the beauty of the Korean language. The late-17th century poet Hong Rang is a particularly stellar example of this:

I send you this willow branch I picked.
Plant it outside your bedroom window, then watch.
When new leaves bud in the night rain, see it as if it were me.

Sijo by Hong Rang

Origins and Development of
Modern Literature (Enlightenment to 1920s)

The beginnings of modern Korean literature can be traced to the country's so-called "Enlightenment" period. It was an era of upheaval that brought a sudden influx of Western modernization into a country that had theretofore been under lock and key, and the tumult is quite evident in the writings of the era's intellectuals. The *sijo* form of the previous generation remained common in the Enlightenment period, but there was a new type of literature taking root, the so-called "New Fiction," which served as a bridge between ancient and modern forms. The writing of this time also incorporated paeans to the wonders of the new culture and to love matches (as opposed to arranged marriages), while addressing issues of social change amid a rapidly changing international environment.

Pyeheo (*Ruins*), *Changjo* (*Creation*), and *Baekjo* (*The Swan*) were the top three literary magazines of the early 1920s.

(Left) First edition of *The Heartless* (Right) Lee Gwang-su (far right) and family with U.S. missionary

Lee Gwang-su was arguably the pioneer of modern Korean literature, his 1918 novel *The Heartless* nothing short of explosive in its impact. First printed in serialized form in a newspaper, it told the story of two young people fascinated by the new culture. The characters, Lee Hyeong-sik and Seo Yeong-chae shed the fetters of traditional society to achieve a new awakening as educators in the new civilization. Over the next decade, in the 1920s, a system took root in which many other people made their formal debuts as writers in the pages of newspapers and magazines.

Lee Gwang-su: All-Around Wordsmith of the 1920s

Lee Gwang-su was one of the most prolific writers in Korean literary history, a famously multi-talented wordsmith whose work included not only short stories and novels, but also devastatingly sharp criticism. His first novel, *The Heartless*, was hugely popular during its serialization in the *Maeil Sinbo* newspaper. It tells the story of young people entranced by the new culture coming into Korea from the West. Protagonist Lee Hyeong-sik is the author's surrogate, a young member of the elite who grew up an orphan but became the focus of his family and friends' hopes. He is hired to tutor Seon-hyeong, a pastor's daughter, and begins to develop feelings for her. But then he is revisited by Yeong-chae, the daughter of his childhood teacher: she is in love with Hyeong-sik, but his heart belongs to Seon-hyeong. After becoming a *gisaeng* and suffering a brutal rape, Yeong-chae resolves to end her life and disappears without a trace, and Hyeong-sik goes out in search of her. Meanwhile, the still-living Yeong-chae meets a man named Byeong-wook and discovers the possibility of a new life studying new literature—here, a character who represents the traditions of the old era develops a passion for the new style of writing. Eventually, the two couples both take part in a recital and a relief effort for flood victims, putting their issues and misunderstandings to bed and resolving to fight for education. Today, this book is viewed as a monument of literary history, one that uses the topic of romance and new ideas about marriage to promote the new values of enlightened culture that were seen as the supreme virtues of their day.

K-Literature Finds Its Footing / Golden Age (1930s and 1940s)

The decades of the 1930s and 1940s saw new and diverse ways of thinking about literature take root as the socialist and national literature strands withered under the Japanese invasion, the subsequent development of colonial capitalism, and the flourishing of urban culture—as well as the harsh policing of thought in response to this urbanism.

The literature of this period was characterized by three major strands:

Lee Tae-jun's *Moonlit Night* is viewed by many as a major contribution to the artistic development of modern Korean literature.

stark realism, a modernist approach centering on values of rationality and individualism, and "pure literature" with an emphasis on aesthetic autonomy and independence. Together, they ushered in the golden age of Korean modern literature. Leading works from this period include Lee Tae-jun's *Moonlit Night* (1934), which achieved a technical peak for the modern Korean novel with its skillful combination of outstanding character observation and description; Park Tae-won's *A Day in the Life of Novelist Gubo* (also 1934), which shows the daily life of an alienated member of the petty bourgeois class against the backdrop of a mid-1930s capitalist city; and Kim Yu-jong's *A Rainy Spell* (1935), a beguiling mixture of farming village lyricism and populist humor.

Park Tae-won: Everyday Life in 1930s Seoul

Seoul: population 10,000,000, Miracle on the Han River, sixth highest population density in the world, 17th highest GDP among world cities. Yet even with this flowery praise, the true face of Seoul remains elusive. In order to uncover what Seoul means in the lives of Koreans, we need to reconstruct its history and customs. In that sense, Park Tae-won's autobiographical novel *A Day in the Life of Novelist Gubo* is a monumental work by a modernist who emphasized sentence-level artistry over ideology and experimented with new fiction techniques without ever losing his emphasis on exploring his characters' internal state. Set in 1934 during the colonial era, the story is of a Korean novelist named Gubo who pens a fascinating novel out of the records of his aimless wanderings around the city of Seoul over the course of a day. If Walter Benjamin spied the light and darkness of civilization in his wanderings around the 1930s imperial capital of Paris, then Park explored the past and future of human civilization as he traveled around the colonial capital of Gyeongseong (today's Seoul).

Day in the Life provides a vivid record of a 1930s Seoul way of life that can only be found in photographs today. It was a decade when old traditions were collapsing and giving way to the new symbols of civilization being built all over the city. Park saw the bygone Joseon era as a "downtrodden old

Park Tae-won and his novel, *A Day in the Life of Novelist Gubo*

Seoul in the 1930s was a mixture of the modern and the traditional.
(Top) The dazzling streets of Myeong-dong (Bottom) The site where people washed clothes

palace" next to the modernity of ever-changing Gyeongseong and its "lively crowds." Old and new coexisted in the city with a dynamic tension. The city was a place of worldly aspirations where "even lyric poets hoped to strike it rich," yet also a place of tradition where women gathered on the banks of downtown's Cheonggye Stream to scrub their laundry and hash over the events of the day. Gyeongseong in the 1930s was much smaller than today's Seoul, but it lacked for almost none of the necessities of a modern city. Packed with department stores, banks, streetcars, and cafés, it provided a clear archetype for the megalopolis Seoul would later become. The character, Gubo, believes he can become a writer by closely examining the Gyeongseong of his own era, the 1930s. *Day in the Life* was a record of the present for Park Tae-won, but for people living in 21st century Seoul, it is a legacy from a past that can never be restored. In the years since its writing, this novel has been a source of inspiration to countless writers and intellectuals, as well as the subject of parodies and theses alike.

Kim Yu-jong

Kim Yu-jong: A Dash of Populist Humor

Kim Yu-jong famously married the lyricism of the farming village to a rich vein of populist humor. His debut novel *A Sudden Shower* relates the story of a woman who stays hopeful despite her poverty, while works like *Bonanza* (1935) and *Plucking Gold in a Field of Beans* (1935) offer a critical and satirical take on the mining boom that was starting to take off in the mid-1930s. Kim wrote around 30 works of fiction before his early death in 1937 from tuberculosis. In particular, the film and television versions of two tales of puppy

(Left) The most recent edition of Kim Yu-jong's masterwork *The Camellias* (Right) Its 1952 first edition

love—*Spring, Spring* (1935) and *The Camellias* (1936)—have become favorites. The former is a tale of first love in which a country bumpkin has to contend with his master's daughter, Jeomsun, and her unrequited love for him. Another master's daughter named Jeomsun can be found a book in *Spring*, a book where the first-person narrator works like a slave—not even being properly paid for his services—as he waits for the chance for her hand in marriage. *Spring* is also an amusing read for its depiction of clashing in-laws. These works share a common thread in their conflicts, namely class difference. The Jeomsuns in *The Camellias* and *Spring* are formidable adversaries to the poor tenant farmer's son in the former and to the bachelor tenant in the latter. In his stories, Kim lets loose with an assured, exquisite display of his ability to address even something as sensitive and controversial as class issues with abundant humor.

Liberation and Division / National Literature
(1950s and 1960s)

Lasting from 1950 until a 1953 armistice, the Korean War has been a mine of material for innumerable writers. It all but took over the local literary community in the 1950s and 1960s; in the years since, many more writers have turned to the conflict as a motif to broaden the scope of their work. Depending on one's political perspective, it has been variously called a tragedy of brothers against brothers, a war to liberate the people, and a proxy war between superpowers. But to the writers of Korea, what it has never been, is a "completed memory" that can be summed up from any one political point of view. The Korean War may have ended more than a half-century ago, but its memories are to many writers an ongoing, forever incomplete experience.

It has, for example, been both a testament to a collective history and a confession of individual recollection. Childhood for these authors was a process of making one's way through a country in ruins. The war was both an impediment to human growth and fertile ground for artistic growth. Their writing has been a struggle with and triumph over devastating trauma. Many authors established themselves with works about the war before going on to enjoy continued popularity for their subsequent fiction, which has frequently been dramatized in film and on television.

Choi In-hun:
A Voice for the Literature of National Division

For many Koreans, the first thing that comes to mind when they think about the terrible Korean War is Choi In-hun's book, *The Square*. The open square is not just a symbol of division, but an ideological symbol that recapitulates

Korean War refugees file across the ruins of a bridge over the Daedong River in search of freedom. The war did great psychological and financial damage to Korea. This picture won the Pulitzer Prize in 1951.

Choi In-hun

the themes of modern Korean history. The crux of the book, which contrasts North and South Korea through the metaphor of open squares versus secret rooms, is that Korean history is not just a topic to be discussed but an encapsulation of the conflicts affecting all modern people.

> *Back when people's secret rooms and open squares were permeable, they were at ease. When kings and commoners had only open spaces, without any secret rooms, the world was at peace. The trouble began when a division opened up between secret rooms and open squares. What do people do when they can no longer find the open squares to ask questions about life?*
>
> *- The Square*

Protagonist Lee Myeong-jun is a university student studying philosophy when he unwittingly becomes a victim of history. Because of his father's political choices, he is driven to the left wing of Korean society. Finally, he makes the decision to cross over into North Korea. South Korea, in its rapid transformation into a capitalist society, feels like a "giant secret room" that pushes people to indulge their personal desires. Heading off in search of a great community symbolized by the "open square," Lee is confronted by a North Korean reality that is vastly different

The Square in English (Left) and Korean (Right)

from his expectations. To his eyes, North Korea is not an "open square," replete with the energy of a liberated community, but rather an oppressive society maintained by orders and obedience. Lee dreams of finding the freedom that he could not experience in the South, but he is unable to find fulfillment on the other side, either.

Finally, he joins the war effort and experiences first hand the clash between the "giant secret room" (South Korea) and the "giant open square" (North Korea). But even in war, he is unable to find a new life purpose. He is captured as a prisoner of war and must make one final choice. Ordered to choose between North and South Korea, the expressionless young man declares that he chooses a "neutral state." The state he refers to is not one that can be found on a map, but the neutral state of his dreams, a place he is destined to never reach (i.e., one in which individual lives are not determined by ideology).

Choi's work continues to occupy an important place in literary history at a time when the division between North and South Korea continues, with fewer and fewer authors showing an awareness of the former's reality.

Industralization, Light and Shadow /
The Desire for Democracy (1970s and 1980s)

The 1970s and 1980s were a time of ideology, when the literature of national division was beginning to take true shape. Works written during this period took a variety of angles on the past and present of a nation divided. Park Gyeong-ri's epic *Land* series (1969–1994) was a systematic attempt to shed light on the history and suffering of the Korean people, following large cast of characters as they confronted fates of hardship and showed insurmountable will in the years from the dawn of modernity through the colonial era and on to liberation. Another tour de force, Jo Jung-rae's *Taebaek Mountain Range* (1983–1989), takes a close look at the national tragedy of war and the calamities it caused. But it goes far beyond simply examining the pain wrought by philosophical difference: it spotlights the history and lives of the Korean people, asking the question of why ideology emerges in the first place, and why people have felt compelled to adopt it.

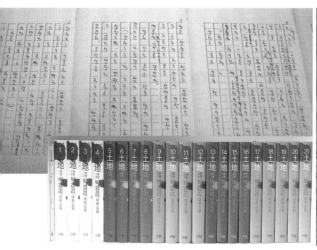

(Top left) A handwritten manuscript (Bottom left) All 16 volumes of *Land* (Right) Park Gyeong-ri

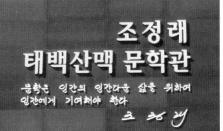

(Left) Jo Jung-rae (Right) A plaque at the literature museum built to commemorate *Taebaek Mountain Range* bears an inscription reading, "Literature must contribute to human beings, so that human beings can live lives befitting human beings."

Meanwhile, the dark side of the so-called "Miracle on the Han River"—the contradictions of capitalist society, the polarization and alienation, the ways in which development squashed the campaign for democracy—had a significant impact on literature. This was a time when the side effects of Korea's light-speed modernization were touching the lives of the public in the most direct ways. Works of literature reflected the lives of the masses struggling with the contradictions of the times, the self-awareness they acquired in the throes of these struggles; and the battle against the system that ensued.

Cho Se-hui is one of the most representative authors of this period. His work *The Dwarf* (1976) offers a dramatic portrait of the conflict between the rich and the poor that dominated the Korea of the 1970s. Moreover, its cyclical structure helped expand the range of possibilities in the novel form.

This period was also something of a dry run for the next, and the fiction that emerged from it showcased a wide variety of trends. Among the books offering a very different take on the development era was *Mama's Stake* (1979) by Park Wan-seo. Park, one of Korea's foremost female writers, offered a sharp critique of Korean social phenomena with beautiful prose and delicately limned psychological portraits.

Cho Se-hui: Alienation of the Urban Underclass

Cho Se-hui first came to the attention of the Korean literary world with *The Dwarf*, an allegory for the plight of the urban poor marginalized in the industrialization process of the 1970s. The book has since seen more than 200 printings, a sign of the great affection Korean readers have for it. It also bears a close connection with the growth of the country's student and labor movements, which sought to understand the underclass lives left devasated by the 1970s industralization drive.

Cho Se-hui and his book *The Dwarf*

The Dwarf was eventually made into a much-loved film version starring renowned actor Ahn Sung-ki. It is also regularly staged as a theatrical production. Recently, it drew renewed attention when Shin Kyung-sook, author of *Please Look After Mom*, said she had practiced as a writer by copying it word for word.

Park Wan-seo: Matriarch of Maternal Literature

Considered one of Korea's foremost female writers, Park Wan-seo uses beautiful writing and delicate psychological shading to present a critical portrait of a vast range of social phenomena, including the Korean War and national division, materialism, and women's issues. Her novel *Mama's Stake* was written at a time when people took it for granted that anyone could succeed through hard work. The mother character in it equates her child's success with her own. Denied the opportunity for a proper education and bereaved of her beloved son by the Korean War, she turns to her daughter to live out her unrealized dreams. The book stands out for its vivid portrayal of a woman who projects her own hopes onto her daughter—motherhood as a symbol not of safeguarding and sacrifice, but of control and oppression.

Park's gift as a writer lies in the way she unsparingly exposes the unexpected torments and unsavory desires lurking underneath the façade of a seemingly perfect—and perfectly happy—middle-class family. The tension in her books stems from the way they lay bare the ghastly selfishness and boorishness of a "model housewife", who to others is the very model of maternity. Indeed, the mother is a recurring focal point in Park's novels; the author excels in showing ambivalent feelings toward an elderly or deceased mother. Her books are something that will privately resonate with every mother and every daughter of the world. In *Mama's Stake*, we find the story of a daughter who only comes to understand her mother by going through the same suffering after losing her—a pain only another mother can know.

Park Wan-seo and her novel *Mama's Stake*

Everyday People /
Something for Everyone (1990s to Present)

The 1990s were a momentous time of reforms and freedom in the former
republics of the Soviet Union. In Korea, too, great changes were afoot.
New trends were taking off in literature and art: an emphasis on personal
wants and a recognition of diverse personal values. It was during this
time that Shin Kyung-sook first established herself as one of the decade's
leading writers with her delicate, lyrical psychological portraits in *Where
the Harmonium Was* (1992). It was also during this time that Yoon Dae-
nyeong made a huge splash with *Silverfish Memorandum* (1994), a novel
that flatly rejected uniformity in favor of a beautifully written exploration
of the individual.

Korean literature was freshly emerging from the "nation" and "society" frames, and female writers in particular were making rapid strides with stories that combined gorgeous prose with an acute grasp of personal feeling. The early 2000s also saw the emergence of more youthful fiction, ebullient expressions of a new way of thinking and fresh sensibility. These works succeeded in capturing readers overseas with their combination of universal appeal and good humor. Finally, this was a period of widespread internet use and sharing of information, phenomena that helped spawn new genres such as "hyperfiction." Writers offered a distinctive new form of fantasy fiction that did not hew to the demands of publishing companies. In just 20 years, Korean literature had achieved both startling diversity and a literary value that stands to help it connect with readers around the world.

Yoon Dae-nyeong: Sensibility of a New Era

Who is Korea's most gifted writer of romantic fiction? Yoon Dae-nyeong would certainly have placed in the top three at any time during the past 20 years. In his older work, romance was not something that budded naturally

Yoon Dae-nyeong and his book *Silverfish Memorandum*

as characters went about their lives—it was a dramatic chance encounter with a total stranger from a faraway place. The lovers in Yoon's fiction fall in lifelong love overnight, confessing all their secrets to this person they have never met before. They pledge eternity on the briefest of encounters. With the 1994 publication of his first fiction collection, *Silverfish Memorandum*, Yoon became an overnight sensation, hailed by the literati as a crafter of "poetic prose" who explored the deepest reaches of human existence. In readers, he triggered a "mythical longing for the origins of being." Indeed, the characters in his books are like those of myth, mysterious and indistinct. Love, in his work, is not an everyday practice, but the dawning of a latter-day legend.

Yoon Sung-hee:
Problematizing the Disappearance of the Family

Yoon's *Spectators*

Yoon Sung-hee has shown an outstanding gift for exploring the meaning and history of the family unit, something contemporary Koreans are increasingly losing sight of. At a time when the expression "family disintegration" has entered everyday parlance, she has shown with her work that the family still holds a vital meaning.

More and more people in Korea today are living by themselves. More lonely souls than ever before live

Yoon Sung-hee

alone, eat alone, sleep alone, and die alone. These people are increasingly alienated from their roots and the family unit. A scant few decades ago, it was commonplace to see three generations under the same roof in Korea; now, the very concept of family is being challenged.

Yoon's novel *Spectators* (2010) tells of a boy who miraculously survives three near-death experiences. It also looks at the way in which the eight members of his family exert profound effects on each other's lives. The boy's miraculous survival owes not to his own luck, but to the efforts of his family, and of all the members of the community who interact with them. The boy may not seem that special, but the stories of his family members are. It is their stories that make him noteworthy as well.

Yoon Sung-hee's writing focuses not on the grand miracles that happen to extraordinary people, but on the everyday miracles that happen to ordinary people. *Spectators* shows the remarkable amount of history behind the birth and life of an ordinary boy, all the connections and love and miracles needed to make that happen. The small but precious miracles that go unnoticed every day are depicted by Yoon with loving care.

Kim Yeon-su:
"Ordinary Lives Make the Most Beautiful Stories"

In the 1980s, Korean novelists turned out stories about political struggles against the obstacles posed by history. Typical subject matter of the time was of people fighting off a despairing reality and striving to scale the

barriers of life. But the 1990s brought a profound change: pent-up human desires flooded the literary scene, like fiery lava spewing from a long-dormant volcano. And in the 21st century, something new has loomed large. People today have no shortage of information, but they find fewer and fewer stories portraying humans in an insightful way. Welcome to the world where everything, even the novel, is deemed a mere commodity.

Kim Yeon-su bucks this trend. He fights to explore what a novel is, what a novel is capable of meaning to people, at a time when not only individual but collective storytelling is fading away. One result of Kim's impassioned efforts is his 2008 book *Whoever You Are, However Lonely You Are*.

No matter how hard people try to escape it, they must eventually face the history of their time. Like love, it shakes off every spurning of its advances, eventually, inexorably reaching its final destination. *Whoever* shows that even a modest personal story can be a beautiful novel. It also demonstrates that individuals cannot live alone, and that their fate is an essential part of a broader history. The novel reveals the secret glue that cleaves together the narrator and others in the web of history: love.

A Historical Treasure Trove for the
'One Source Multi-Use' Age

Koreans in general are keenly interested in historical dramas. Indeed, if you ask someone to think of a famous figure from Korean history, the first name that comes to mind may well belong to the actor who played him or her on television. Recent years have also brought another new trend: "historical fiction as therapy." Here, modernites seek solace in their contemporary woes by watching the sadness and inner conflicts of personages from history. By sharing and understanding these feelings, they look for a way to resolve the problems that plague them today.

Historical fiction is more than just entertainment, though. It also offers education: readers whose appetite has gone unsatiated by textbook tidbits look to it for new ways of interpreting history from their own perspective. Adding to the appeal is the fact that in addition to historical information, they can also pick up a wealth of detail on the language, customs, and culture of the day. All of this has helped make historical fiction one of the most noted developments of the so-called "info-tainment" era.

Miniseries are wildly popular in Korea, and historical fiction provides a treasure trove of source material. The evolution of the genre has marched in tandem with developments in the "K-Drama" industry, resulting in a burgeoning market for historically themed fiction.

There was no shortage of historical fiction before the 2000s. But while those works were typically viewed as "popular fiction," more recent works have blurred the lines with pure literature. The opening salvo in this renaissance came courtesy of Kim Hoon and his 2001 book *Song of the Sword*.

(Left) *Song of the Sword* chronicles the heroic exploits of Admiral Yi Sun-sin, who saved Korea from an invasion by Japan in the late 16th century. (Right) *Hansandaecheop-do* is a depiction of the battle where Admiral Yi led his forces to triumph.

Sword is a chronicle of the exploits of Yi Sun-shin, the admiral (and figure of national adulation) whose heroics helped save Joseon era Korea from a Japanese invasion in the late 16th century. The novel was praised at the time for marrying mass appeal with literary merit. A hallmark of Kim's writing is its meditative prose style, and *Sword* was also enthusiastically received for its first-person narration of Yi's battle and triumph.

Another big hit with readers was Kim Young-ha's *Black Flower* (2003), which brought a sophisticated new approach to familiar subject matter. The book was based on an episode from a century before, in which the first Korean immigrants to Mexico were sold off to a henequen plantation by imperialists who coveted their homeland. Kim uses his characteristic animist imagination to give an entirely new spin to a story with which most Korean readers are well acquainted. *Black Flower* shows that historical fiction is not just about ancient history—it can also connect with the most cutting-edge cultural sensibility to produce something never before encountered.

(Left) Korean and French editions of *Black Flower*, a story about Korea's first immigrants to Mexico
(Right) Korean workers carrying cacti at a Mexican farm in the early 1900s

(Left) *The Deep-Rooted Tree* tells the story of Hangeul as a mystery.
(Right) As a miniseries, *The Deep-Rooted Tree* was popular for its strong story structure and performances.

With historical fiction enjoying a boom in public attention, a growing number of writers have begun dedicating themselves exclusively to the genre. Perhaps the most successful has been Lee Jung-myung, whose *The Deep-Rooted Tree* (2006) brought mystery novel techniques to the story of the creation of Korea's Hangeul writing system by King Sejong the Great, a figure viewed by many Koreans as the greatest monarch in the nation's history. Lee's work was a triumph of wedding the allure of historical fiction to the best qualities of the detective genre. The author also penned *The Painter of Wind* (2007), which applies a modern twist to another well-known historical personage, folk artist Sin Yun-bok. In his book, Lee explores the possibility that Sin, a beloved figure for his genre paintings, may have actually been a woman.

Both *Tree* and *Wind* were adapted into hugely successful miniseries—another part of Korean historical fiction's ongoing transformation in its profitable partnership with mass media.

The Painter of Wind was about Sin Yun-bok, a famous folk artist of the Joseon era.

Chapter Three

REACHING OUT TO THE **WORLD**

Trends and Achievements in K-Literature Abroad

Korean literature first began making its way to overseas audiences in the late 19th century. Hong Jong-u, the first Korean exchange student in France, arrived in Paris in December 1890 and worked for almost two years as a research assistant at the Guimet Museum. While there, he devoted himself to producing French translations of astrology texts and classic works of Korean fiction like *The Story of Chun Hyang* and *The Story of Shim Chung*. He was also shown in newspapers dressed in traditional *hanbok* clothing and with his hair in a *sangtu* topknot, drawing notice as an enlightenment politician from the kingdom of Joseon. He collaborated with the Frenchman J. H. Rosny on a translation of *Chun Hyang* that was eventually published under the title *Fragrant Spring*. His translation of *Shim Chung* likewise played a major role in bringing Joseon culture to European readers.

As an exchange student in France, Hong Jong-u was the first to share Korean literature in translation.

But it was only after the 1922 publication of *The Cloud Dream of Nine* in Britain by the Canadian missionary James Gale that Korean literature really began receiving attention overseas. Gale had a strong enough command of Korean to publish Korea's first-ever English-Korean dictionary, and he contributed a number of books on Korea and Korean grammar for foreign readers. *Cloud Dream* is a classic of Korean fiction that captures the unique sentiments and lifestyle of the country's people. Other examples of Korean works being introduced to foreign readers include the 1940 publication of a Joseon fiction collection in Japan and the 1947 release of a translation of Kim Nam-cheon's novel *Daeha* in Czechoslovakia.

Up until the 1960s, published translations came primarily from the Korean canon. It was only in the 1970s that modern literature began seeing translation and publication through various channels. The 1980s were when overseas publication really began to take off. Before then, publications had very often been classics that Korean scholars or missionaries translated out of scholarly interest or as an introduction. But from the '80s onward, active efforts were made to translate Korean literature in its modern form.

In 1974, the Korean Culture and Arts Foundation began providing support for the translation of Korean literature. *Stars*, a collection of short fiction by the well-known writer Hwang Sun-won, was published in 1980 by Hong Kong's Heinemann Asia. This marked the beginning of a prolific period of exchange with the global literary community, with various forms of institutional support made available for translation and publication. As of September 2011, an estimated 1,564 works had been translated into 34 languages and published in 52 countries. The largest number (292) were English translations, with another 224 in Japanese, 221 in Chinese, and 214 in French. In addition to these four languages with over 200 translations each, there were also 171 translations into German, 96 into Spanish, 94 into Russian, and 59 into Czech. The list goes on: Italian (29), Polish (21), Swedish (16, of particular note because of the Nobel Prize), Bulgarian (15), Romanian (10), Turkish (9), Hungarian (7), and Dutch (6) in Europe, as well as Vietnamese (25), Mongolian (8), Hindi (6), and Urdu (4) in Asia. With each day, the list of languages and countries grows ever longer and more diverse.

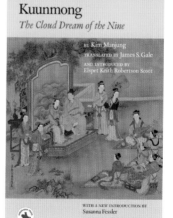

Canadian missionary James Gale and a modern edition of *The Cloud Dream of Nine*, which he translated and published in Britain in 1922.

The Investigation
Snags Pre-Pub Export Deal

Recently, one particular novel drew a lot of attention when its worldwide English publication rights were sold to a leading publishing group—a first for a work of Korean writing, and a sign of the new Korean Wave in literature. *The Investigation* (2012) was written by Lee Jung-myung, a writer of popular historical fiction. The mystery novel centers on the death of a Japanese censor who burned the works of Yun Dong-ju, a famous Korean poet and independence activist. An investigation into a homicide at a Fukuoka prison in the late stages of the Pacific War uncovers a most foul conspiracy by Japanese militarists involving the jail and an escape attempt by its prisoners. A work of heartwrenching humanity, *The Investigation* has its basis in the tragic real-life story of Yun, who died in a Fukuoka prison in 1945 at the age of 27—a victim of horrifying vivisection experiments conducted on prisoners. It is both a work of fiction centering on a person whose life intersects with

The main character in this novel is Yun Dong-ju, a famous Korean poet and independence activist.

the grand narrative of history, as well as a humanist war novel that shows how the madness and disillusionment of war cannot kill off hope.

Noted overseas agents and editors said the book was both a gripping read

with the pace of a mystery thriller (thanks to its investigation plotline) and a work of great literary merit that dwells on such weighty themes as humanity, barbarism, war, and justice. Maria Rejt, an editor at Pan Macmillan (the British company that acquired the rights), praised it as a rare masterpiece with a consummate mixture of literary quality and popular appeal, and expressed confidence that it would live up to its billing as one of her company's main titles. The hardcover version is scheduled to come out in spring 2014.

The Public-Private Connection

LTI Korea and the Daesan Foundation

Since 1996, the Literature Translation Institute of Korea (LTI Korea) has been working in various ways to help Korean literature reach the rest of

the world through translations, overseas publishing, and creative support. Its efforts include developing translations that resonate with overseas readers, building an infrastructure for the globalization of Korean literature and Korean books, and establishing a network of authors, translators, and publishers.

The Daesan Foundation has earned renown not just for translations of existing Korean literature but also for its unstinting support for the writing of new works. It uncovers new talents and outstanding work through various literary awards, and it actively contributes to the globalization of Korean literature by offering various opportunities for writers to broaden their horizons. In particular, a support program established in 2010 for the translation, research, and publication of outstanding examples of Korean writing—a key effort in the globalization of Korean literature—has been operating in combination with a literature research project.

The LTI Korea and Daesan Foundation websites also offer excellent opportunities for foreign readers to get a systematic, in-depth introduction to Korean literature. (LTI Korea: http://eng.klti.or.kr/e_main.do, Daesan: http://daesan.or.kr/eng/)

Working to Share K-Literature

Translators hold a special place for their contributions in bringing Korean literature to the world. Recent years have brought changes to the old system in which it was primarily Koreans translating into English. More and more often, people from various countries are working to translate Korean writing into dozens of the world's languages.

One especially noteworthy translator is An Jeong-hyo. Himself a well-known novelist, An has devoted many years to the translation of Korean literature. Indeed, he has drawn praise from critics in the U.S. for his work in English. His *White Badge* (1983) was actually published in the U.S. before it came out in Korea; *Silver Stallion* (1990) was given a simultaneous release in both countries. Film versions of his work have also been warmly received overseas, including adaptations of the two abovementioned novels and

(Left) English edition of *White Badge*
(Middle) English edition of *Silver Stallion*
(Right) An Jeong-hyo

The Life of Hollywood Kid (1992). An is proficient both at translating Korean literature into English and at translating foreign literature into Korean. He has also channeled his wisdom into a guide for translators called *Translation Attack and Defense* (2006).

Meanwhile, a number of foreign translators have settled in Korea and made it their life's mission to translate its literature. One excellent example is Na Su-ho. Born Charles La Shure in the United States, he majored in English literature back home before coming to Korea in 1995, where he fell in love with and married a Korean woman, settled down, and adopted a Korean name. Now a professor at the Hankuk University of Foreign Studies Graduate School of interpretation and translation, he began his translating career in earnest with a 2003 award from LTI Korea as best new translator for his version of Jeon Sang-guk's *A Planaria*. He spent the year between March 2005 and March 2006 working on an English translation of Kim Young-ha's *Black Flower*. Whenever asked why an American would study Korean literature or take a Korean name, Na has simply replied that he likes Korean literature—that it's like asking which is better, vanilla or chocolate ice cream. Tastes cannot be explained in logical terms. In addition to his work translating Korean writing into English, he is also very interested in studying the history of Korean literature, collaborating on an English translation of Jo Dong-il's *Korean Literature in Cultural Context and Comparative Perspective*.

There have also been success stories of Koreans and foreigners collaborating on translations. This kind of work offers the chance for the globalization of Korean literature to become a true meeting of cultures, rather than a one-way "introduction" from one to the other. One standout team is the Korean-Russian pairing of Kim Tae-ok and Vladimir Ivanitsky.

Translators and Their Love
of Korean Literature

Brother Anthony of Taizé: *Heung* and *Han*

British-born Brother Anthony earned a master's degree in English literature from Oxford University. Today a monk with France's Taizé Community, he took on a position as a professor in the Sogang University Department of English Language and Literature in 1980, a post through which he shared translations of Korean poetry and fiction in Britain and the U.S. A naturalized Korean who adopted the name An Sonjae (taking his motif from *Little Pilgrim*, which he

translated in 1991), he has since retired and devotes himself exclusively to translation. His interest in Korean literature was first sparked when he was exposed to a lot of it around the time of the 1988 Olympics in Seoul. He began his translation work at the urging of acquaintances. His 1990 version of Ku Sang's *Wastelands of Fire* was praised as enjoyable and ably translated. He went on to publish translations of collections by master Korean poets (Ko Un's *Ten Thousand Lives*, Seo Jeong-ju's *The Early Lyrics*) in the U.S. and U.K. Also an avid reader of fiction, he has translated such novels as Yi Mun-yol's *The Poet* and *The Son of Man* and Ko's *Flower Ornament Sutra*. He has been recognized for his ability with a translation prize at the 1991 Korean Literature Awards, as well as a 1995 Daesan Literary Award for his English translation of *The Poet*. Allen Ginsberg raved about his ability after reading *Beyond Self*, a translation of Zen poetry by Ko. The noted Beat poet said Brother Anthony's translation was outstanding, and that he offered a good model for American poets.

Brother Anthony points to the characteristic Korean emotion of *han* (a collective sense of resentment or sorrow) as one of the reasons Korean literature is able to resonate with the readers of the world. Readers, he said, sense the humanity of the *han* that appears in Korean poetry, discovering the characters as people who strive to never give up and to live like human beings despite the torment and anguish of it all. In his view, foreign readers understand and enjoy Korean literature because they also experience the same things in their lives. Even the "developed" countries of the world, he says, are bound to have poverty, oppression, and the pain that results.

Kevin O'Rourke: First Foreign Doctor of Korean Literature

Today an emeritus professor at Kyung Hee University, Kevin O'Rourke arrived on Korean shores in 1964 as a priest with Ireland's Columban Mission Society. A lover of literature since his seminary days, he went on to earn a master's degree in Korean literature in 1970 and a doctoral degree in 1982, eventually landing a position teaching students at Kyung Hee University. In addition to his educational career, he has also contributed to global awareness of Korean literature with his translation work since the 1960s, including ancient verse in the *sijo* style and an English version of Choi In-hun's *The Square*. He has published more than 20 books of Korean literature translated into English, including a collection of Korean poetry in the 1980s, a volume of verse by Seo Jeong-ju in the 1990s, and a version of Yi Mun-yol's *Our Twisted Hero* in 2001. The first of these in particular was

honored with a prize for outstanding translation by London's Poetry Society. On Hangeul Day (October 9) in 2009, he was honored with a Bogwan Cultural Medal from the Korean government for his contributions to the advancement of Korea's written language. And in 2010, he had the O'Rourke Library dedicated in his name by the Irish embassy in Korea in recognition of his services as a cultural bridge between Korea and Ireland.

(Left) American Na Su-ho (born Charles La Shure) is a professor at the Hankuk University of Foreign Studies. His love for Korean literature led him to settle down in Korea.
(Middle) Na's translation of Kim Young-ha's *Black Flower* (Right) Kim Tae-ok and Vladimir Ivanitsky spent their own money to publish a translation of the modern Korean poetry they loved.

Together, they have worked on publishing modern Korean poetry from the 20th century in Russian translation. Kim, who holds a Ph.D. from Moscow State Pedagogical University, does the first draft; Ivanitsky, a specialist in Eastern literature, does the "literary version." Their work includes Russian translations of collections by Korean-Russian poet Kim So-wol and Choi In-hun's novel *The Square*, but they have also been the first to share leading 20th century modern poets with Russian readers. The pair first teamed up on translating the century's poetry after a chance meeting at a barbershop. They started doing it for fun, out of a mutual love of modern Korean poetry, but their translations soon found their way into print, bringing the two closer together in their bonds of friendship. Because of copyright issues, they had to shoulder the costs for a Russian publication of *Twentieth Century Korean Poetry*, a work five years in the making. In an environment where most Korean literary translations have been spearheaded by the LTI Korea or the Daesan Foundation, their translations are arguably all the more historic for being completely independent.

Global Interchange

Since the dawn of the new millennium, great changes and developments have been afoot in the Korean literary community's approach to the rest of world literature. Before then, it hewed to the most basic and classic forms of cultural exchange: foreign translations, as well as authors visiting countries before publication for readings, meetings with readers, and interviews with the press.

But the period since the 2000s began has seen a more diverse, even revolutionary approach to actively sharing the whole of Korean literature with readers abroad and creating a new discourse in world literature where Koreans themselves are active participants. In the process, there has been a fundamental shift—from Korean writers simply learning about the literatures and cultures of the world and incorporating new trends via foreign writers and prominent international authors to a relationship of mutual influence and adoption, where writers share views on an equal footing as they exchange their literary visions and cultural trends.

Writers take part in an opening day discussion at the 2nd World Literature Forum in Seoul in 2005. From left: J. M. G. Le Clézio, Yu Jong-ho, Luis Sepúlveda, Hwang Sok-yong.

Korean and international writers were invited to Seoul in 2011 for the 3rd World Literature Forum.

Andrew Motion
이문열
박범신

정현종
은희경
Liu Zaifu

한강
유종호
Terry Jaensch

J.M.G. Le Clezio
정과리
김우창

Gao Xingjian
구효서
최원식
성석제

Ana Maria Shua
최재천
도정일

김치수
Zack Rogow
Ben Okri

Ingo Schulze
정지아
김연수

송병선
최윤
이인성
정이현

조경란
복거일
김경욱
곽효환

김인숙
김성곤
Shimada
Masahiko

World Literature Forum in Seoul

The World Literature Forum in Seoul is an event that invites major names in world literature to join leading Korean writers in discussing contemporary themes. The first event, which took place in September 2000 under the theme "Writing Beyond Borders," had around 20 of the world's top writers and poets attending, including Wole Soyinka, Pierre Bourdieu, Margaret Drabble, Gary Snyder, Karatani Kojin, and Ismael Kadare. A second event in May 2005 focused on "Writing for Peace." Nineteen major names in world literature—Kenzaburo Oe, Jean Baudrillard, J. M. G. Le Clézio, Orhan Pamuk, Bei Dao, and Mo Yan among them—joined Korean writers in analyzing the causes of conflict and war throughout the global village and discussing the role literature can play in ushering the world into an era of greater peace and prosperity. A third event on life and writing in a globalizing era came in May 2011: for three days, attendees looked at the topic of globalization, something that has, for better or worse, become an inseparable part of our lives, and examined its momentous impact on lives great and small and on our spiritual world. Fourteen major figures in global literature were invited, including Nobel laureates Le Clézio and Gao Xingjian, along with Ben Okri (considered one of Africa's most influential voices), Andrew Motion (a former Poet Laureate of Great Britain and one of the judges for the Booker Prize), and Antoine Compagnon (one of the great thinkers in Europe). The forum brings together 50 to 70 major Korean and overseas literary figures over a one-week period for a rare opportunity to talk about crossing borders, visions for peace, and issues of globalization.

2005 Frankfurt Book Fair Guest of Honour

Korea's status as Guest of Honour for the 2008 Frankfurt Book Fair afforded its writers a valuable experience in interacting with the European literary community over the course of a year. In addition to the publication of Korean works by top German publishing houses, writers also gained confidence in their ability to communicate by impressing an awareness of Korean literature and culture on European readers. The fair kicked off with an opening speech by Ko Un; the following day, the *Frankfurt Rundschau* daily printed one of his poems in both German and its original Korean. Indeed, a total of 1,769 articles about events associated with Korea's honor were printed in the German press between October 2004 and December 2005 thanks to the book fair—around 5 to 10 percent more than the

Ko Un gave a celebratory address at the opening of the 2005 Frankfurt Book Fair, where Korea was Guest of Honour.

average for the previous Guest of Honour. This media attention went a long way in helping to bring Korean writing to the rest of the world.

East Asia Literature Forum

Active efforts are also under way to organize interactions with Korea's neighbors and countries with similar historical experiences. The East Asia Literature Forum had its inaugural event in Seoul during its founding year of 2008; two years later, a second event was staged in Kitakyushu, Japan, with a third scheduled to take place in China in 2012. The organizers of this forum hope to see its literary exchanges bear fruit with the development of shared East Asian values and a vision for the region's future. This is especially crucial in the East Asian region whose countries have been locked for centuries in a close relationship of mutual influence, yet also have a dark legacy of modern history and the still-smouldering embers of conflict. The forum was developed as a way of moving past all of this, bringing intellectuals and artists from the three countries together in an ongoing search for more future-oriented values and a vision for peace. It is attended by some of Korea, China, and Japan's most prominent

The first East Asia Literature Forum was held in Seoul in 2008.

mainstream writers and thinkers, with each country contributing its own organizing committee from trusted organizations to work together on the event. Observers are looking ahead to see what the future will bring.

In addition to the events mentioned above, there is also the International Writers' Festival, organized by LTI Korea to promote interaction between Korean and global writers, and the Paju Bookcity International Publishing Forum, for which the Bookcity Culture Foundation invites officials from the world's top publishing houses to look at trends in the global publishing market and seek out ways for Korean literature to communicate more efficiently and meaningfully with the world's readers.

Today, interchange between Korean and global literature and international experience for Korean writers are more active and far-reaching than ever before. These events, which provide outstanding opportunities for close interaction, are expected to lay solid groundwork for more active and meaningful discourse between Korean and global literature in the years to come.

Korean Influences on
World Literary Greats

J. M. G. Le Clézio, the French writer who won the 2008 Nobel Prize in Literature, has a great affection for Korean writing. He spent a year in Korea as a guest professor at Ewha Womans University in Seoul, during which time he gave readings with local writers. Professing a love for Korea's byways and subways, Le Clézio has published poetry about Korea, as well as a short story set in the country. While talking with reporters in Seoul after the Nobel Prizes were announced, he noted that there were a number of Korean writers worthy of Nobel honors, pointing to Anatoli Kim, Hwang Sok-yong, and Lee Seung-u as his personal picks.

Meanwhile, Kenyan writer Ngugi wa Thiong'o is said to have written *Devil on the Cross* (1982) after being bowled over by the Korean poet Kim Ji-ha's "Five Bandits." Indeed, unbeknownst to many Koreans, Kim's work was having a major impact on Kenyan readers: at one point, students were expelled for staging a play based on it.

(Left) J. M. G. Le Clézio, winner of the 2008 Nobel Prize in Literature
(Right) Kenyan writer Ngugi wa Thiong'o

Chapter Four

WRITERS AND WORKS WITH A GLOBAL FOLLOWING

Ko Un and *Ten Thousand Lives*

Looking Through 2,000 Years of History to Show the Korean People's Past and Future

Ten Thousand Lives is a tour de force by Ko Un (1933–), a figure who has gained renown as a master poet not just in the Korean literature community but around the world. His reputation stems from the way he places the universe we inhabit—the lullabies of the sea, the whispers of life, the gestures of trees—into his socially engaged verse. *Lives* is a monumental work 30 years in the making. Ko first began developing it in 1980 when he was in prison for his democracy campaigning; it was published in parts between 1986 and 2009, with the completed version only seeing print in 2010.

The finished product contains 4,001 pieces. Poets around the world called it one of the most extraordinary conceptions in contemporary literature. As its title suggests, it is a "verse encyclopedia of people."

Ko Un's
Major Works

Going to Munui Village (1974)
Early Morning Road (1978)
Little Pilgrim (1991)
Flowers of a Moment (2001)
Ten Thousand Lives (1986–2010)

And *Lives* is something the poet himself holds a great affection for, as evidenced by his decision to take eight months after its 2009 completion to verify its historical accuracy and correct any mistakes with the names in its more than 4,000 parts. The result could well be called a poetic register of the Korean people; one critic described

Ko Un's *Ten Thousand Lives* consists of 30 volumes and took 30 years to complete.

it as the sound of the waves from a great river—"a song about people"— coursing out to the vastness of the sea.

The first part of *Lives*—which the poet said "proceeds from the basic environment of my childhood"—explores the history of a village and its warm, neighborly inhabitants, who remain full of good cheer despite decades of dire poverty. The middle portion, released after a seven-year hiatus, sees the poet focusing his verse on the 1970s, with such noted Korean literary figures as Shin Gyeong-rim and Paik Nak-chung making an appearance on its pages. It also includes prominent references to historical figures esteemed for their virtuous character, including former Presidents Kim Dae-jung and Roh Moo-hyun and the Buddhist monk Beopjeong. In the last poem of Volume 30 ("The Boy in the Cave"), Ko sings of life—the inexhaustible stone books, stone songs, and stone stories of the eons:

Because of you, this world is full of sunsets,
this world's long-lasting long stories will never end.
This evening too the stories
of ten thousand lives, of people's living and dying, will have no end.

Yi Chong-jun and *This Paradise of Yours*

Salvation for the Suffering in a World of Absurdity

Yi Chong-jun (1939–2008) was the rare example of an author who knew how to seamlessly blend issues of history and philosophy into his literature. His novels, which focus on the scars of traumatic experience and their meaning, have been hugely popular in their written and film versions, the latter including Im Kwon-taek's screen adaptation of *Seopyeonje* and Lee Chang-dong's *Secret Sunshine*, based on *A Story of a Worm*.

Yi's masterwork, *This Paradise of Yours* (1976), chronicles the turbulent

lives of people living around a leper colony. Its backdrop is the Sorok Island Hospital (a facility for those who suffer from Hansen's disease) in the years after 1961, when a coup brought a military administration into power in South Korea. Col. Jo Baek-heon, the newly appointed medical officer, selflessly devotes his

Korean edition of *This Paradise of Yours*

mind and muscle to making this desolate island a paradise, only to see his efforts end in failure. In his book, Yi uses the theme of building paradise to present a serious discussion of that universal vision, a result of human desire. While Jo's one-man crusade may fail, the writer suggests that divided people can unite and work together to create the utopia of their dreams—an idea epitomized in the conclusion, in which the conflicting characters choose to return to Sorok Island. Through their decision to

Yi Chong-jun's
Major Works

The Wounded (1966)
This Paradise of Yours (1976)
Ieo Island (1976)
The Cruel City (1978)
Seopyeonje (1993)

work together to build their paradise, Yi is expressing the universal dream of a true utopia not just for any one group, but for all of us.

Human history has seen endless attempts at creating utopias, yet most of its pages are filled with disgrace and oppression, for those utopias were paradise-as-ideology, a means of control and oppression that thwarted the individual desires of the people living under those systems. As a consequence, history buries away the question—what kind of country is paradise?—in a morass of falsehood; heaven is something that can never arrive. The meaning of *This Paradise* lies in the way it uncovers the true, illusory nature of that paradise and suggests instead a real utopia, one that everyone agrees to search for a way of finding. It can also be found in the way the book uses a suitable mode of storytelling to embody this theme.

Translations of works by Yi Chong-jun: French edition of *This Paradise of Yours*, English edition of *The Wounded*, French edition of *Iodo*

Hwang Sok-yong
and *The Old Garden, Shim Chong*

Realistic and Insightful Portraits of Young Lives

The battle for democracy holds a special meaning in Korean history, and the writer Hwang Sok-yong (1943–) incorporates its battlegrounds into works of literature. Hwang has earned great renown for his continued evolution through action and practice, and for his reflections of that world in his work. Active as a writer since 1962, he showed his determination to reach the public with a message of political defiance in *The Old Garden* (2000), and broadened his scope of interest into East Asian history as he tackled the theme of the heroic aura of the woman in *Shim Chong* (2003).

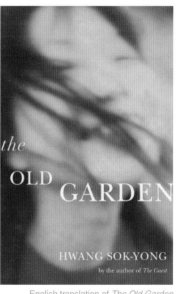

English translation of *The Old Garden*

The Old Garden is a story of the turbulent lives and love of a man and woman, set against the backdrop of a South Korea in upheaval and the collapse of the socialist world order in the 1980s. Protagonist Han Yun-hee criticizes a century tainted by absolute patriarchal power and bureaucracy; she is a fervent believer in recovering the "maternal love for the masses" described by Rosa Luxemburg. Through this character, Hwang searches for hope in the quiet introversion of the mother, the figure who bears and cares for us all.

© Hwang Moon-sung

Hwang
Sok-yong's
Major Works

A Chronology of Mr. Han (1972)
The Land of Strangers (1974)
The Old Garden (2000)
The Guest (2001)
Shim Chong (2003)

The Old Garden has been published in many languages.

The book's ideas of restoring a lost maternity are further developed in the character of "Cheong" in *Shim Chong* (2003). Shim Cheong is a staple character in Korean classical fiction, a model of the pious, self-sacrificing daughter who sells herself to restore her father's lost eyesight. Hwang transplants this character into a modern setting with Cheong, a far more assertive and active figure than the Shim Cheong familiar to most Koreans, an individual situated in a specific context of life and history. She may sell her body to survive, but she does not bargain with her heart; she says that *she* will choose the men, rather than being chosen by them. The Cheong in Hwang's novel does not break before the father who used and abandoned her. She withstands the abuse and violence of men who see her solely as an object of desire and exploitation. Nor does she lament her fate of having to sell herself to stay alive. She only comes to understand the true meaning of life when she cares for others who are suffering and lonely like her, or more so. She takes in dozens of babies born to prostitutes who could not support them; she works to save up money to help the poor. And she takes out beautiful revenge against a world that never cared for her by showing an infinite ability to care without condition or calculation. Hwang once put his pen to writing histories of triumph; the ones he writes today are histories of love, mercy, and caring.

Yi Mun-yol and *Our Twisted Hero*

Captivating Readers with Prose and Erudition

Yi Mun-yol (1948–) is widely appreciated by Koreans for the storytelling gifts he shows in addressing a wide variety of subjects and themes with gorgeous prose and consummate erudition. He also boasts the largest number of works in translation of any Korean author.

His best-known work may be *Our Twisted Hero* (1987), a satirical take on the rise and fall of the powerful, set in a small-town elementary school during the final days of the Liberal Party administration. The narrator, Han Byeong-tae, transfers there from Seoul when his public servant father is demoted. He finds himself in an empire of power, the creation of crafty young dictator Eom Seok-dae. Byeong-tae suffers a severe crisis of values and decides to put up a lone resistance, but he soon realizes the futility of it all and ends up allying himself with the powerful. He is basking in this sweet sense of authority when a new teacher arrives at the school, bringing a revolution to a place where no democracy seemed possible. The Eom regime is destroyed—but, Byeong-tae realizes, its tyrannies were not ended by the oppressed children themselves. Had it not been for the new teacher, the students would never have had an opportunity for reflection and realization. The class struggles through trial and error under the new regime, gradually establishing a new democratic order.

English translation of
Our Twisted Hero

Years pass. Now an adult living in an absurd world, Byeong-tae looks back and feels an odd sort of nostalgia for the Eom Seok-dae days. Then,

Yi Mun-yol's
Major Works

The Son of Man (1979)
A Portrait of Youthful Days (1981)
Our Twisted Hero (1987)
An Anonymous island (1988)
The Poet (1991)

The Poet, another masterwork by Yi Mun-yol, has also been translated into multiple languages.

while taking a summer vacation, he happens to see the now-grown Seok-dae in handcuffs, being dragged off by police.

The novel takes the form of the narrator's reminiscence on the past. He was the only one to stand up against Seok-dae, but he is also keenly aware of his inability to do anything to stop the abuses. This sort of intellectual nihilism forms a strong undercurrent to the novel. By presenting Byeong-tae as a character with a complex personality, it injects a note of realism, focusing on the narrator's interpretation of Seok-dae rather than the dictator's "twisted life." In the process, it successfully transcends the limitations of what could easily have come across as a conventional allegory for the inevitable downfall of an immoral tyrant.

Oh Jung-hee and *The Bird*

Exquisite Language and a Meticulous Reflection on Human Themes

Oh Jung-hee (1947–) plumbs the depths of the human psyche with exquisite language and meticulous character studies. She is especially adept at bringing out the sadness, fear, anxiety, and loneliness of women, a characteristic present in her work since she debuted in 1968 with *The Toy Shop Woman*. Her books have given tragic shape to the desires and emotions of women hemmed in by a patriarchal system.

Oh's tour de force may be her 1996 novel *The Bird*, which adopts the perspective of a young girl as it examines the arduous lives of a brother and sister abandoned by their parents. The world reflected in the eyes of its 12-year-old protagonist is an endless parade of hardship and pain. She and her younger brother live an isolated life in a small apartment in a poor neighborhood. Their father, a construction site laborer, has left them alone to search for the girlfriend who ran out on him. Their neighbors also come from the ranks of the poor and unfortunate. One, named Jeong, is wanted for murder; Yeon-suk, daughter of the elderly landlady, lives with the agonies of disability; and a couple of factory workers are persecuted for their homosexuality.

English translation of *The Bird*

'Delicate, understated writing that finds the extraordinary in the ordinary.' Tobias Hill

THE BIRD
OH JUNG-HEE

Oh Jung-hee's
Major Works

Evening Game (1979)
Garden of Childhood (1981)
The Bronze Mirror (1983)
Spirit of the Wind (1986)
The Bird (1996)

(Left) Polish translation of a short fiction collection by Oh Jung-hee, and the first Korean printing of *The Bird* (Right) *The Bird* has been translated into numerous languages. In 2003, it was awarded the LiBeraturpreis, one of the biggest literary honors in Germany.

The main symbols in the book are the bird and bird cage of the children's neighbor Lee. The boy dreams of becoming a bird and flying away, but like the caged bird, he cannot escape the mire of his misfortune.

> *"The day is light, and the night is dark. But the hour between when the sun sets and before the night arrives, this uncertain, and ambiguous darkness, that which comes in waves, filling the space between heaven and earth and stifling our heart, to which I cannot give a name; how it is different then and now, what flows between it all, I cannot explain."*

In 2003, *The Bird* became the first work of Korean literature honored with a LiBeraturpreis, one of the biggest literary honors in Germany.

Lee Seung-u and *The Reverse Side of Life*

French Favorite Invites Readers on a Journey inside Themselves

Lee Seung-u (1959–) has been described as a writer who "invites readers on a journey inside themselves." He is more popular in France than in his home country, a fact that is perhaps owing to the Kafkaesque world in his work being more familiar to European readers. Yet his writing is unsettling even for those familiar with the Czech author's dualistic perspective on the absurdities of life. His work is a discomfort that stems from Lee's focus on the fundamental guilt within the human mind.

All of us are capable of unwittingly committing a crime against another. Often, we feign ignorance even after being made aware of it. By the time we unconsciously realize our misdeed and try to atone for it, it is too late. This is the psychology that Lee delves so trenchantly into.

Lee Seung-u's *The Reverse Side of Life* has been published in various languages.

Lee Seung-u's
Major Works

The novel *The Reverse Side of Life* was first published in 1992. Its structure involves the author-narrator investigating the life of a novelist named Park Bu-gil. The narrator has been asked by a magazine company to write an account of Park's life, a respected literary figure. Using interviews with Park and his autobiographical fiction, he reconstructs the writer's life. Park's writing focuses on his own unhappy home life and the woman he once loved. He grew up in his uncle's house, where a lunatic was caged in the backyard; the madman kills himself with nail clippers passed to him by the boy. Park subsequently learns that the madman was actually his father. Wracked with guilt, he runs away and becomes a drifter. One day, he meets a missionary from a church in his hometown. With the missionary's help, he finishes high school. By chance, he meets an older woman named Jong-dan and falls in love with her. She encourages him to attend church, and when she says she wants to marry a minister, he decides to go to seminary. But she eventually leaves to study overseas. Learning that he has been abandoned, Bu-gil quits university for a solitary existence. Eventually, he decides to become a writer.

By reconstructing the "reverse side" of the life of novelist Park Bu-gil through a book by another author-narrator, the book offers a meticulous examination of how the darker aspects of life are both concealed and revealed in a person's writing.

Korean editions of *The Reverse Side of Life* and *The Private Lives of Plants*

Shin Kyung-sook and *Please Look After Mom*

Moving Readers with Delicate, Lyrical Psychological Portraits

Shin Kyung-sook (1963–) established herself as one of Korea's top writers in the 1990s with delicate and lyrical psychological portraits that have resonated strongly and generated a fervent following with countless readers. As an author, she is famous for the wholehearted devotion she brings into her writing process. And with her 2006 book *Please Look After Mom* (released overseas in 2008), she scored Korean literature's best sales of the new millennium.

Please won readers over with its story of a selflessly devoted mother who suddenly goes missing. It touched off a veritable "Mama mania" back home, bringing the topic of the family in 21st century Korea to the fore. In recent years, more and more Koreans have found themselves fighting a lone battle, without anyone to support them. A collapsing social safety net and retrograde social service policies have fanned an increasing anxiety

Korean editions of works by
Shin Kyung-sook:
(Left) *Deep Sorrow*, her first novel
(Right) *Please Look After Mom*

Shin Kyung-sook's
Major Works

Where the Harmonium Was (1993)
Deep Sorrow (1994)
A Lone Room (1995)
The Train Departs at 7 (1999)
Please Look After Mom (2008)

among people who believe they have no one in the world to turn to for protection. The stratospheric rise of the country's economy since the 1970s was brought to a shuddering halt in 1997 as the foreign exchange crisis dealt a blow that rippled throughout society. Out-of-work fathers found their economic power and prestige rapidly slipping away; in the collective unconscious, there was a growing sense that only mothers were left. *Please Look After Mom* is a portrait—troubling, sad, stirring—of this "new matriarchy."

Some critics contended that the book, and Korean society in general, goes too far in turning the mother into a sacred or mythical presence. If everyone in the family relies on the mother, who does she turn to when she is in need? *Please* reminds readers that there is another, unseen side to the mothers who devote their lives to the family, awakening them to the simple truth that mothers need mothers too—that they are people, women, who need the absolute love of another. Even critics of the mindset that takes the all-sacrificing mother for granted have admitted to being brought to tears by Shin's book. Such is the indelible image of the mother in Korean minds: an object of compassion, the only person who can be trusted and relied on in this world. What has made *Please* a cause célèbre for the 21st century is the way it shows both the limits and the possibilities of the Korean image of the family.

Please Look After Mom has been printed in the U.S. (Top), Great Britain (Left), and Japan (Right).

Kim Young-ha
and *I Have the Right to Destroy Myself*

An Urbane Sensibility and a Flair for Humor

Since making his debut as a writer in 1996, Kim Young-ha (1968–) has been praised for portraying the urbane sensibility of Korea's younger generation with dry wit and an objective gaze. His fiction offers vivid portraits of contemporary young people with a characteristic sense of humor, a combination that has resonated strongly with younger readers in Korea, America, Europe, and Asia.

His first and best-known novel, *I Have the Right to Destroy Myself* (1996), is narrated by a so-called "suicide designer" who assists others in taking their own lives. It is the rare example of a work of Korean literature centering on the theme of death, and the storyline itself was a shocker: the idea of a character whose "job" is to help other people die was something unheard of in Korean fiction. Drawing writers and readers into a world of weird and chilling fantasy, the book ended up taking top literary honors back home.

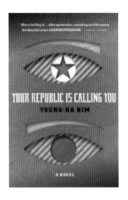

Other major works by Kim Young-ha in English translation: *The Black Flower, Empire of Light*

Kim
Young-ha's
Major Works

I Have the Right to Destroy Myself has been published in numerous languages.

Kim points to three "symptoms" of contemporary life: death, sex, and narcissism. In *I Have the Right*, the emphasis is squarely on the first one of these. Fittingly, the narrator teaches suicide methods to people who want to die and helps them out with the necessary procedures. Once the deed is done, he goes on a trip and writes fiction to chronicle their short lives. In the book, he assists two people: Se-yeon (Judith) and Mimi. Other characters include siblings C and K, as well as "she," the Hong Kong woman whom the narrator meets on a trip to Vienna. Life for them is no less painful than death. Hypocritically, they position life and death as diametrical opposites, going over the top in extolling the former. As Kim puts it, if the modern day gives everyone all they need to choose death, then the narrator provides the lure:

> There are only two ways to become a god in this day and age: create or kill.

> Human beings today live without purpose. All they need is a sufficient motive for death, not even a necessary one, and they kill themselves. [...] More than anything else, the modern person's death impulse speaks typically to the symptoms of modern life; by showing this kind of pathology of life, I was trying to express the absurd situation we encounter here and now.

Our ability to decipher this shocking declaration from the novel may be the key to understanding *I Have the Right to Destroy Myself*.

New Writers and Works
to Take Note of

As Korean literature has gained stature around the world and more and more international editors and readers have taken note of it, attention has been shifting from its established greats to its newer voices. While the previous generation of modern Korean writers explored such weighty themes as the war and the resulting decades of a divided country and separated people, or the historical consequences that countless people were forced to suffer through, today's younger writers are looking to more idiosyncratic themes for their work. They focus on universal subject matter with an appeal in the global market, showing commercial savvy while captivating critics and readers alike with powerful narratives, creative imagination, and convincing structure. Below is a list of some more recent books that have yet to see print overseas, but that are drawing attention from both the local literary community and the foreign publishing market.

Kim Ae-ran, *My Palpitating Life*

Kim Ae-ran has an almost magical ability to take the most minor incidents and give them cosmic proportions. Her work shows that a consummate grasp of details offers one way of perfecting the whole. Her trademark fast-paced prose pulls the reader deep inside her settings in the space of just a few sentences. Considered one of the most magnetic role models to aspiring young writers today, Kim writes novels that resonate widely—a fellow writer once said that she "puts the moves on everyone, men and women, young and old." *My Palpitating Life* uses the life and death of Areum, a 17-year-old boy with progeria, to offer a beautiful and moving exploration of what it means to grow old or "act your age."

Kim E-seol, *Welcome*

Kim E-seol's fiction does more than just offer a dazzling display of dreams and fantasy or an abstruse exploration of the interior world. Rather, it goes straight to the very concept of reality. Is happiness something distributed equitably to each of us? How long are we capable of bearing the misfortunes that get piled on us? In *Welcome*, Kim looks at the lone struggle of a woman who takes

responsibility for her family in lieu of her ineffectual husband. The writer offers an objective portrait of how a woman triumphs over destiny in a world that offers no shred of salvation or hope.

Jeong You-jeong, *A Night of Seven Years*

Jeong You-jeong is one of the main figures in Korean "middlebrow" fiction today—she might be called the country's answer to Stephen King. Her books are loved by readers for their fast pace and gripping narratives, their breathless mystery structures, and the author's worldview, which remains objective without losing its warm human touch. Jeong came to notice for *Spring Camp*, about an ordinary boy's escape from a mental hospital, but it was *A Night of Seven*

Years that catapulted her to best-sellerdom, with its vivid rendering of the internal feelings and desires of the different people associated with a murder case. With their realism, imagination, and outstanding crime scene depictions, Jeong's books are already on their way to the big screen.

Uniting Over Beautiful Differences

As the internet and social media develop, the people of the world are dealing with more information than ever before in human history, and on a daily basis. But no amount of changes in mass media can do much to alter the natural function of literature. It invites us to experience hitherto unknown lives; it takes us deep inside places and times we have never encountered before. It helps us travel outside spatial and temporal borders, beyond boundaries of race and nationality, to a place where we commune with the invaluable experiences and wisdom of humanity, past and present.

The globalization of Korean literature is not merely about bringing Korean books to the countries of the world. It has a crucial role to play in building a future back home where Koreans are able to live together with people of different nationalities. Now more than ever, it has become the norm for Koreans to live side by side with people from all over the world. Korea is home to more than 200,000 multicultural families, whose members have either found employment in Korea or married a Korean; indeed, such families frequently appear in works of Korean writing. Popular examples include Kim Ryeo-ryeong's *Wandeuki* (a big hit in its film version) and Park Bum-shin's *Namaste*. The question of how so many different people can learn to understand their differences and truly live together has become more pressing than ever. Literature can do a lot to help the people in this social environment bridge their differences and avoid conflict. So globalizing Korean literature is about more than just exporting Korean books—it is about creating an environment where the people of the world can share their true feelings.

Recent years have seen the burgeoning of the "one source, multi use" (OSMU) environment—a single novel may become a TV series, film, play,

and even a musical. As the cultural environment changes rapidly, Korean fiction has been adapted into content for a wide variety of media, gaining new possibilities for reaching a wider audience. And its reach could be broader still, when more active use is made of literature's inherent potential: the force of a beautiful sentence, the powerful desire to communicate, the hope of making people happier. This is the engine that will power Korean literature in the century to come.

Further Reading

Books on K-Literature

Peter H. Lee, *Anthology of Korean Literature: From Early Times to Nineteenth Century* (1983), University of Hawaii Press

Peter H. Lee, *Modern Korean Literature: An Anthology* (1990), University of Hawaii Press

Kichung Kim, *An Introduction to Classical Korean Literature: From Hyangga to P'Ansori* (1996), M.E. Sharpe

David McCann, *Early Korean Literature* (2000), Columbia University Press

Bruce Fulton, *Modern Korean Fiction: An Anthology* (2005), Columbia University Press

Lee Namho ... et al, *Twentieth Century Korean Literature* (2005), EastBridge

Suzanne Crowder Han, *Korean Folk & Fairy Tales* (2006), Hollym Intl

Marshall Pihl, *Land of Exile: Contemporary Korean Fiction* (2007), M.E.Sharpe

Peter H. Lee, *A History of Korean Literature* (2009), Cambridge University Press

Jesse Russell & Ronald Cohn, *Korean Literature* (2012), Book on Demand Ltd.

Websites on K-Literature

Literature Translation Institute of Korea (LTI Korea)

http://eng.klti.or.kr/e_main.do

The Daesan Foundation   http://daesan.or.kr/eng/

Korean Modern Literature in Translation http://www.ktlit.com/

Korean Authors' English-language Websites

Ko Un   http://www.koun.co.kr/default.html

Shin Kyung-sook http://www.facebook.com/KyungsookShinAuthor

Kim Young-ha http://kimyoungha.com/english/bio.html

Korean Publishers' English-language Websites

Changbi Publishers, Inc. http://en.changbi.com/

Moonji Publishing Co, .Ltd. http://moonji.com/english/greetings/

Munhakdongne Publishing Group http://www.munhak.com/english/index.asp

ABOUT THE AUTHOR
Jung Yeo-ul

A literary critic, Jung graduated from Seoul National University in German literature before earning her Ph.D. there in Korean literature. She currently has a regular feature, "Jung Yeo-ul's Humanities for Young People," in the *Hankyoreh* newspaper, and has contributed writings on literature, the humanities, film, and television to the *Dong-A Ilbo, Cine21, GQ Korea, Publishing Journal,* and *list: Books from Korea*. She is also actively involved in work for the public, giving lectures and developing books on literature and the humanities to help people better understand the fields. Her other books include *Jung Yeo-ul's Fiction Reading Time, Jung Yeo-ul's Literary Mentoring, Cinephile Diary, Communication, Media Arachne,* and *A Young Lady Finds Hope in the Forest of Popular Literature*. She has also translated the book *Korea Between Empires, 1895–1919* into Korean.

CREDITS

Planner   Global Communication and Contents Division
Writer   Jung Yeo-ul
Translator   Colin Mouat

Edited & Designed by Seoul Selection

Photographs

Yonhap Photo, Newsbank Image, The Associated Press, Korea Tourism Organization,
The Daesan Foundation, LTI Korea, Moonji Publishing Co,.Ltd, Changbi Publishers, Inc.,
Lee Kwa-yong